A souvenir guide

Tyntesfield
Somerset

M000167485

National Trust

Rise, Decline and Rediscovery

'I feel quite confident in saying that there is now no other Victorian country house which so richly represents its age as Tyntesfield.'

Mark Girouard, *The Victorian Country House*

Tyntesfield's story is the rise, decline and rediscovery of an outstanding Victorian country house and estate. Created by William Gibbs, the richest commoner in England in the mid-1800s, it is a statement of prosperity and confidence, fervent faith and family fortunes.

Where there's muck…

Built on overseas trade, the Gibbs family business expanded dramatically when they started importing guano from Peru in 1842. Guano, or dried bird droppings, revolutionised Victorian agriculture and horticulture, providing rich fertiliser suitable for large- and small-scale use. William Gibbs rapidly became immensely wealthy. A committed Christian, he spent his fortune funding churches and charitable work and on improving his family home. In 1863, when he was 72, he commissioned Bristol architect John Norton to enlarge and remodel the house on the Tyntesfield estate. Redesigned in High Victorian Gothic style, richly decorated and furnished by leading craftsmen, Tyntesfield became a remarkable Victorian country house.

A remarkable survival

Each of the following three generations left their mark on Tyntesfield, but kept the estate running as a unit. Each generation made changes to the house and estate, but these were achieved with sensitivity, adding to and not undoing the work of their predecessors. It is this that makes Tyntesfield so fascinating – the house, Chapel, servants' quarters and most of their contents as well as the formal and kitchen gardens, Home Farm, estate buildings, farmland and woods have survived largely intact. Collectively, they reveal the lives of four generations of the Gibbs family and the people who made Tyntesfield work. They demonstrate the changing tastes and shifting practicalities of life in a country house, recalling Victorian and Edwardian heydays as well as the slow decline typical of many country houses in the 20th century.

Declining fortunes

When guano deposits were exhausted by the 1860s, the firm diversified into nitrates, copper, bark, tin, silver wool and into shipping and merchant banking. However, the 1929 Wall Street Crash and subsequent Great Depression of the 1930s caused business to suffer. Income gradually declined, and various, largely unsuccessful, attempts were made to generate money from the Tyntesfield estate.

The Second World War of course took its toll, as the manpower required to run the estate was not available. But the Gibbs family, ever part of their community, welcomed boarders from Clifton High School to the house, and also made Tyntesfield a Red Cross distribution centre, while American soldiers convalesced in temporary hospitals on the estate.

When Richard, the last Gibbs to live at Tyntesfield, took over the management of the house and estate, he focused on the maintenance of the gardens, Kitchen Garden and the immediately surrounding land. He lived alone, with none of the household staff that had once greatly outnumbered the family, and use of the house gradually shrank into fewer and fewer rooms. By the time Richard died unexpectedly in the summer of 2001, the main reception rooms were mostly shuttered and closed up, but kept well ordered.

A reversal of fortune

Tyntesfield's fortunes changed in 2002 when the National Trust acquired the house and core of the estate through generous public donations and grants, initiating an ambitious and ongoing programme of conservation and repair, actively supported by local people.

Opposite Tyntesfield approached from the east, taken in 1902

The Gibbs family

Four generations of the Gibbs family lived at Tyntesfield between the 1844 and 2001. The house was the family's much-loved country home, where they lived and gathered for celebrations and events.

Tyntesfield's creator

William Gibbs (1790–1875) was the man who created Tyntesfield. He and his wife Matilda Blanche (1817–87) lived first in London, where their seven children were born. With a growing family and business booming, they looked for a country residence. The Gibbses had relations in Bristol and Gloucestershire, and the opening of the Great Western Railway in 1841 may have also influenced the decision.

Above A Gibbs family celebration, early 20th century. The inscription above the door translates as 'Peace to those who enter, health to those departing'

Left William and Blanche Gibbs with five of their seven children; painted by Sir William Ross in 1849

William bought the original late-Georgian house in 1843 and 20 years later hired John Norton to redesign and rebuild it as a beautifully appointed family home. Norton doubled its size, creating a splendid country house built in the High Victorian Gothic style.

William and Blanche enjoyed more than 35 years of marriage; their letters and diaries reveal great affection and humour. Both deeply religious, they funded many churches including Keble College chapel (see page 25). After William's death, Blanche continued these charitable works, funding scholarships and community buildings.

When William bought the Tyntesfield estate he sought to enhance and enlarge it. Over the next 20 years he bought the adjoining Charlton estate, and other nearby properties to increase his landholding and to provide his sons with homes.

Antony Gibbs

Antony (1841–1907), William's eldest son, did not join the family business, preferring the life of a country gentleman. He married Janet Louisa Merivale in 1872 and they spent the first 18 years of their married life at Charlton. Antony was a talented craftsman, particularly interested in the arts and architecture as well as technology and design. He built Home Farm and managed the estate. When he inherited the house after his mother's death in 1887, he altered and modernised it using the latest technology, including electricity.

George Gibbs

George (1873–1931), Antony's son, inherited Tyntesfield in 1907. A successful and influential politician, he became the 1st Lord Wraxall in 1928. He and his wife Via redecorated some of the house, reflecting Edwardian tastes. Via died in 1920, leaving a daughter, Doreen. In 1928 George married the Honourable Ursula Lawley, daughter of the 6th Baron Wenlock, who then became the 1st Lady Wraxall.

They had two sons, Richard and Eustace. Tragically widowed after just four years, Ursula ran the house and estate on behalf of Richard until he came of age in 1949.

The last Gibbs at Tyntesfield

Richard (1928–2001), 2nd Lord Wraxall, never married. After a career in the army at Sandhurst and in the Coldstream Guards, he returned to Tyntesfield, where he joined the North Somerset Yeomanry and later the Territorial Army. He devoted the rest of his life to managing the house, Kitchen Garden and estate, where he lived alone until his death in 2001. His will left the estate to 19 beneficiaries, bringing about the sale of Tyntesfield.

Above The 1st Lady Wraxall, Ursula Gibbs, with her sons Richard and Eustace; by John Arthur Machray

Arrival at Tyntesfield

In 1866 William Gibbs finished rebuilding his house in the High Victorian Gothic architectural style and was ready to welcome visitors and impress them with his vision made real.

Imagine arriving at Tyntesfield as a guest in 1866. Travelling in a horse-drawn carriage, you enter the secluded wooded valley catching tantalising glimpses of a large honey-coloured stone building. It is a glorious High Victorian Gothic mansion with a multitude of elaborate windows, turrets, gables and spires surmounted by a richly patterned clay-tiled roof. Until the 1930s there was a magnificent clock tower soaring above the entrance doors. Then, as now, arriving at Tyntesfield was awe-inspiring.

Clevedon Lodge

Points of entry

In William's time there were five entrances with lodges. Different lodges were used according to the destination – Clevedon Lodge for a journey to Clevedon, Clifton Lodge for Clifton. The North Drive was not the main entrance to the house in William's day. Then most visitors arrived via the South Drive, which offered a more impressive arrival at the front of the house, surrounded by its gardens, parkland and woods.

Opposite The roofline of Tyntesfield bristling with Gothic turrets and chimneys

Above One of the many gargoyles that cling to Tyntesfield's Gothic façade

Below The entrance to the South Drive, decorated to receive a wedding party

Today most visitors to Tyntesfield arrive at the northern entrance, Clevedon Lodge, and drive down the valley through the double avenues of lime and golden yew trees towards the house and Home Farm.

All the land surrounding the North Drive is part of the Tyntesfield estate, although that owned today by the National Trust, 218 hectares (539 acres), is only the central portion of the original estate, about a quarter of the land owned by William Gibbs in the 1860s.

Automatic gates

A gateman and his family lived in Clevedon Lodge, which was built in the picturesque Gothic style. Originally the gates were wooden and were opened and closed by a winch inside the porch, so that they appeared to operate automatically.

Today's impressive metal gates, with the St Kilda ram and the coronet of the Wraxall coat of arms, were installed in 1968, a 40th-birthday present from Ursula, 1st Lady Wraxall, to her son Richard.

Home Farm

Antony, William's eldest son, built Home Farm in 1881. It is a fine example of a late 19th-century model farm, planned for optimum efficiency and productivity. Model farms developed in the late 18th and mid-19th centuries, but it was highly unusual to build one during the severe agricultural depression of the 1880s and 1890s.

Antony was particularly interested in managing the estate and built Home Farm before he inherited. However, Antony did not rely on farm income – the family business had ample funds to invest in Home Farm. It was a dairy farm, with a prize-winning herd of Alderney cows.

Antony's son, George, 1st Lord Wraxall, was an eminent politician who left estate management to his agent. By the late 1930s a large flock of laying hens had built up.

Poultry proved a valuable commodity, especially during the Second World War, providing eggs and meat for the house and also to outlets including shops in Clifton, Bristol.

When Antony died, Ursula ran the estate until her eldest son Richard came of age. Richard, 2nd Lord Wraxall, maintained the estate for more than 50 years, until his death in 2001.

Above Antony Gibbs, every bit the country gentleman, with his hunting dog and gun

Left Tyntesfield's poultry flock appears to have been large enough to be commercially viable by the end of the 1930s

A busy, noisy place

The courtyard was the core of Home Farm, full of people, animals and activity. Many of the tools and equipment needed for the farm and estate were made or mended here in the carpenter's workshop, paint shop, mason's yard, sawpit and forge. Machinery in the courtyard was powered by a huge steam traction engine. A slaughterhouse and butchery near the milking parlour prepared meat for Tyntesfield and the Gibbses' other households.

The buildings' layout exploited the sloping land, with gravity helping to move animal feed. Fodder was brought to the courtyard at the higher level for processing and then fell down chutes to the milking parlour and animal pens below.

Changing uses

As with all farm buildings, Home Farm's use has altered over time, as agriculture has adapted to meet new demands. Built as a dairy farm, the buildings have also been used to rear pigs and hens. Agricultural use finally ended in 1991. In 2010–11 major changes were made at Home Farm, sensitively and imaginatively converting the buildings into permanent visitor facilities, offices and accommodation for staff and volunteers. Farming and forestry continue on the estate, managed by National Trust tenant farmers and staff.

Core of the estate

William and his descendants gradually accumulated more than 1,215 hectares (3,000 acres) of land along the Land Yeo River valley. The Gibbses' continued ownership preserved this rural wooded landscape for over 150 years. The subsequent purchase in 2002 of the core of the Tyntesfield estate by the National Trust guarantees its survival for the future. This peaceful countryside is all the more remarkable for being just seven miles from Bristol city centre.

Left A Victorian photograph of the estate team at Home Farm

Below Tyntesfield's prize-winning herd in the parkland

The Chaplain's House and Lodge

The Gibbses had their own resident chaplain, which was quite unusual in Victorian times, but very much in keeping with William and Blanche's deeply held Christian faith.

William and Blanche were both keen supporters of the Oxford Movement, which was also known as Tractarianism. (For more information on the Oxford Movement and Tractarianism see page 25.) We know there were at least two resident chaplains at Tyntesfield: the Reverend John Hardie was employed by William Gibbs in the 1860s and by Blanche after William's death; the Reverend John Medley was Antony's chaplain.

Daily worship

The chaplain had a central role in daily life at Tyntesfield and was considered part of the family. In William's time, morning and evening prayers were held in the oratory, a devotional room that he had commissioned John Norton to create within the house (see page 25). In the last years of his life, William decided to build a private chapel and, once completed, family prayers and services were held here. Sadly William died before the Chapel was finished, but Blanche and later Antony attended daily prayers there.

Opposite Chaplain's Lodge
and the adjoining
Chaplain's House

Double doors

The porch of the Chaplain's Lodge has two doors, one on each side, facing up and down the drive. Inside, another door leads into the gateman's house and would have been used by the gateman when he was operating the gate. The two outside doors allowed pedestrians to travel along the drive without opening the gate. Estate staff recall how useful these side doors were at the other lodges, especially when they returned late after a night out: 'You could just go straight through the two side doors and didn't have to wake the gateman – very handy!'

Separate lodgings

Chaplain's Lodge and House are on the North Drive. Chaplain's Lodge, on the right, is the older building. It was built in the 1840s, in a simple Tudor Gothic style, and was originally a gatekeeper's lodge, marking an entrance to the estate. The adjoining, grander Chaplain's House was built by Antony between 1889 and 1891, for Reverend John Medley. It is more imposing, built in the Gothic Revival style with two floors looking onto the drive and a lower floor used by servants. It was probably designed by architect Henry Woodyer, who undertook alteration and modernisation work for Blanche and then Antony.

Holiday cottages
Both the Chaplain's House and the Lodge were
refurbished in 2009–10 and are now, along with
Summerhouse Cottage, holiday cottages available for
rent. For details visit www.nationaltrustcottages.org.uk.
They are occasionally open to visitors.

Tyntesfield Plantation

Tyntesfield Plantation is a 21-hectare (52-acre) woodland stretching along the top slopes of the Failand Ridge, giving the house a delightful wooded setting when viewed from the south.

Probably part of the original estate that William bought in 1843, Plantation was improved and extended by William and his son Antony. They planted more trees and created new paths, rides and glades lined with specimen beech, yew, box and cedar trees. Their work enhanced the setting of the house and added to its privacy. Plantation was used for recreation and forestry. The family enjoyed walking, riding and shooting here and it also provided timber for the estate and house.

The Summerhouse

The Summerhouse is at the western edge of Plantation, above Bendle Combe. A single-storey octagonal stone building with a pyramidal roof, it has a south-facing rustic verandah and, when built in the 1860s, would have had distant views over the Bristol Channel before the surrounding trees matured. The Summerhouse faces south and was used for summer lunches and shooting parties, with all the food, drink, cutlery and crockery being brought up from the house to be served to the family and their guests by the butler and footmen. Ursula, 1st Lady Wraxall used to bring her grandchildren to the Summerhouse for tea parties and picnics in the 1960s and 70s. It was restored in 2009-10.

Above The parkland, Plantation and surrounding countryside seen from the roof of Tyntesfield

Left The recently restored Summerhouse

Opposite The Sawmill has a new function as a learning centre

The Sawmill

Around 1889 Antony built the brick Gothic-style engine house with its great arched doors and the accumulator room with a glazed lantern roof in the former quarry. The engine house had steam engines that generated electricity for the house, still a novel technology at the time. The open-fronted building to the right, probably a former quarry building, was used as a coal store. When mains electricity was brought onto the estate in 1952, the engine house and accumulator room were no longer needed. The coal store was converted to a sawmill and still contains its 1950s machinery. The engine house and accumulator room were repaired and converted into a learning centre in 2008, which now welcomes thousands of adults and children every year.

Supporting Tyntesfield

In its heyday, in Victorian and early Edwardian times, Tyntesfield was home and workplace to more than 150 people. The magnificent house and estate functioned as a single, efficient entity, incorporating the best craftsmanship and most innovative machinery of the day.

Below From left to right: George Gibbs on 'Sir Brian', his sisters Anstice on 'Weston' and Albinia on 'Success' and brother John on 'Boomerang'

Keeping the estate moving

Stables were vital elements of all country estates, as horses were the main source of transport and power. In 1837 there was 'a coach house and Stables' on the site. In William's time, Tyntesfield's equestrian facilities were relatively modest. It was Antony who developed and modernised them.

The Stables

In 1888 Antony commissioned architect Henry Woodyer, who added more stables, a heated harness room and new staff accommodation. He created an impressive entrance to the original stableyard, with tall metal gates hung on high ornamental stone piers. Other new features included wrought-iron lanterns and a central horse trough with a fountain and sundial. Woodyer also built the archway into the second courtyard, where he added a house and harness rooms.

Antony's stables were modern, spacious and built to very high standards, with fittings by specialist suppliers St Pancras Ironwork Company. Two stables in the second, inner courtyard were used as sick bays. The coach house in this inner courtyard accommodated six carriages. In the 20th century, as cars replaced horses, two of the coach houses were extended to form motor houses or garages. The petrol pump was installed in 1957, supplying fuel for the family's cars and other estate vehicles.

Above The stone sundial and horse trough in the stable courtyard designed in 1888 by Henry Woodyer

New residents
The former hayloft in the Stables is now a maternity roost for the extremely rare greater horseshoe bat.

Feeding the estate

The scale, completeness and continuous productivity over almost two centuries make Tyntesfield's Kitchen Garden remarkable. Its layout has scarcely changed since the 1890s and it retains nearly all the buildings and features from that time.

The Kitchen Garden

This garden has never stopped supplying fruit and vegetables for the house since William's time in the 1860s. It continues today, with the garden providing fresh produce for the restaurant and cafés.

The whole area was extensively remodelled by Antony in the 1890s. He commissioned the Arts and Crafts architect Walter Cave to redesign the garden in the newly fashionable English 'Wrenaissance' style, inspired by buildings such as Christopher Wren's Hampton Court Palace. The remodelling included the construction of extensive ranges of glasshouses, an orangery, a decorative new entrance with a small walled flower garden (known in the mid-20th century as Lady Wraxall's Garden) and a cut-flower garden as well as working buildings including an office,

Above The bothy and Orangery, photographed by *Country Life* in 1902

Below The Kitchen Garden walls have eyes – through which training wires are threaded to support fruit trees

apple store, tool shed, boiler room, potting sheds and a bothy to house junior gardeners. A coal boiler heated water for an efficient network of pipes that heated the glasshouses and cold frames.

When the work was completed the cut-flower garden was renamed the Jubilee Garden to commemorate Queen Victoria's Diamond Jubilee in 1897. The Jubilee Garden and Lady Wraxall's Garden served as decorative rather than productive areas for the family and their guests to enjoy, and were linked to the house by paths through the gardens and park.

Productive and efficient

The Kitchen Garden was astoundingly productive and efficient, and it was the duty of the head gardener to ensure that the best fruit, vegetables and flowers were grown. 'State of the art' metal Victorian glasshouses produced vines, figs and pineapples as well as apricots, peaches and nectarines. Fruit trees grew against the walls inside and outside the walled garden, which also produced vegetables. Soft fruit and root crops were grown outside the walled garden in the 'slip gardens', which were less protected from wind.

The Orangery

When the National Trust acquired Tyntesfield, the Orangery was virtually derelict with several stone columns missing and serious damage to the roof. Students from the Architectural Stone Conservation course at the City of Bath College are taking part in a three-year training programme which enables them to work one day a week to restore and conserve the grand façade of the Orangery.

Top Dahlias in the Jubilee Garden in front of some of Walter Cave's Arts and Crafts inspired buildings

Right A melon in its 'cradle' ripening in one of the Kitchen Garden glasshouses

Powering the estate

Although Tyntesfield estate has always enjoyed a bounteously rural setting, it lacked the facilities to support Antony's programme of modernisation. So a number of ambitious engineering projects were implemented to support and drive the estate's growth.

Tyntesfield's water supply is a typically ingenious Victorian solution to a problem. There are no natural streams on the estate, so all the water required for the house, Home Farm and other buildings had to be either pumped up from the river valley or captured as rainwater and stored. Amazingly these original water supplies are still in use today, and provide water for the gardens and cattle troughs. Tyntesfield was not connected to mains water until 2008.

When William bought Tyntesfield in 1843, water from the Land Yeo River and a well in the valley was pumped up an underground main through the estate to a huge underground holding tank on the adjoining Charlton estate. Powered by gravity, a network of underground pipes supplied the house, estate and Home Farm. Water even powered a service lift (see page 35).

Top right The engine house that once powered the house

Right One of Antony's greatest achievements was his solution to Tyntesfield's water supply

Water from the skies

Rain was the other source of water for the house and estate and this was captured at the Water Catch and from the roofs of the main buildings. The Water Catch is one of Tyntesfield's more unusual features. It is a large rectangular 'field' above Plantation, covered with a layer of asphalt. Rainwater was caught by the impermeable asphalt and piped down to the house for the water closets, baths and fire hydrants. Rainwater was also piped from the roofs of the main buildings into underground storage tanks, for use in the house, gardens and farm buildings.

Turning on the gas

In the 1860s, the house, estate offices and lodges were lit by gas which was supplied by the estate's own gasworks near the Kitchen Garden. Gas was also used in the kitchens. Coal was burnt at high temperatures, producing inflammable gas that was stored and used for lighting, heating and cooking. Apparently the Gibbs family imported coal from northern England as they thought local coal made inferior gas. It travelled by boat from Liverpool to Bristol Docks and was carted out to Tyntesfield. The gasworks probably ceased operating in the late 1800s, when Antony installed electricity around 1889. The building became the estate office and is now offices for National Trust staff.

Self-generated electricity

Antony installed electricity at Tyntesfield in 1889-90. An engine house and accumulator room were built in a former quarry in woodland close to the Chapel. Two steam engines generated electricity which was stored in two banks of storage batteries – the accumulators. The walls of the accumulator house were lined with glazed bricks to prevent the battery acid from damaging the structure of the building.

A leading light

Tyntesfield was an early example of a country house generating its own electricity. When it was first installed, Antony spent the night alone in the house, checking that 'this new fangled electric light' was safe and suitable.

Above A decorative lantern in the main entrance that would have been gas-powered before Antony installed electricity in 1890

Daily Life and Worship

Tyntesfield was the family home of four generations of Gibbses, from 1844 to 2001. Each generation made alterations but kept many of the original furnishings and fittings, giving us a rare insight into life in this magnificent Victorian country house.

Nothing but the best

The architectural design and building work William and Blanche commissioned for Tyntesfield, and the alterations and modernisation undertaken later by their son Antony, all incorporated the latest Victorian technology and involved the finest craftsmen of the time. Together they created a family home that was comfortable and efficient as well as being an impressive Victorian country house.

Declining fortunes

After George, 1st Lord Wraxall died, his widow Ursula worked tirelessly to maintain Tyntesfield, but the estate no longer provided the income to support the lifestyle the family had previously enjoyed. Numbers of staff working in the house and on the estate declined throughout the 20th century, and when Richard, 2nd Lord Wraxall died in 2001, there were fewer than 10 people employed at Tyntesfield. Richard never married and, as the years went by, he gradually closed and shuttered many of the rooms to protect their contents.

Opposite William, Blanche, their seven children as well as the house chaplain, John Hardie. *c.*1862

Left Details such as this lion's-head light-fitting combine craftsmanship and technology, with a touch of the playfulness of a family home

A generous and dutiful family

William and Blanche enjoyed a long and happy marriage, and although they became extremely wealthy as the family firm flourished, their lifestyle remained relatively modest, reflecting their devout Christian beliefs. They were generous benefactors, funding numerous churches and almshouses in London, Exeter and Bristol as well as buildings for their workers in Wraxall. Their sons continued this charitable work, funding many religious and educational projects including the hall, library and common rooms of Keble College at Oxford. All four generations of the Gibbs family were committed to their staff and local community, serving as Justices of the Peace and Lord Lieutenants and supporting national and local charities.

A dedicated man

The most impressive and moving monument to William Gibbs is in the church he had built in Exeter, his home town. There, his marble effigy depicts him with a flowing white beard, clad in his night shirt and clasping a bible. It is inscribed: *William Gibbs, a merchant of London, but by parentage and affection a man of Devon, in his life did many good works for the love of Christ, as elsewhere, so especially in the city of Exeter. One such work – the erection of the Church of SS. Michael and All Angels for the use of the poor of the neighbourhood – is here recorded by his widow and surviving children, to the end that the remembrance of his loving kindness and piety may not pass away.*

Rooms for family and friends

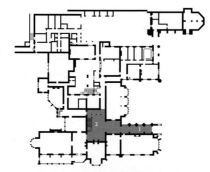

Visitors would be received via the Cloister into the grand, full-height Hall. Also in daily use was the Library, used as a family sitting room. The Organ Room is a small space but one that was central to life at Tyntesfield.

1 The Cloister

In William and Antony's time, the second set of doors with decorated hinges were the front doors. George, Antony's son, added the outer door in the early 1900s. All visitors came into the house through the intensely Gothic Cloister. Designed by John Norton as part of William's remodelling, the Cloister gives an impressive entrance through a series of bays with vaulted ceilings supported by finely carved stone pillars. The floor is patterned with plain and encaustic tiles made by Minton, the leading Victorian tile manufacturer.

A royal visit

Queen Mary came to Tyntesfield in 1939 when she was visiting Bristol in connection with Red Cross work. Ursula, Lady Wraxall, was closely involved with the Red Cross and had been the Queen's Maid of Honour for several years before she married George.

'Ugly house with some nice pictures & things & a fine view from the Terrace….'

Queen Mary on her visit to Tyntesfield in 1939

2 The Hall

In 1889 Antony commissioned architect Henry Woodyer to create a more imposing and spacious circulation route that enhanced the guests' 'journey' from the Hall to the Drawing and Dining Rooms. Woodyer removed Norton's glazed screen that had separated the Cloister from the Hall and added carved stone doorways to the Dining and Oak Rooms. Before it was redesigned, five of the downstairs rooms had opened off the Hall.

Designed to impress

The Hall in the centre of the house was an important reception area, designed to create a sense of awe and grandeur for visitors (it is 43 feet [13 metres] from the floor to the ridge beam in the roof). It formed the hub for access to all the areas of the house for the family. Tyntesfield's Hall is magnificent, with cantilevered stone stairs rising to galleries leading to the first-floor family bedrooms, the whole space crowned by a carved wooden Gothic lantern roof created by John Norton.

Opposite left **A monkey carved in stone above the door to the Cloister in the porch**

Opposite right **The Cloister**

Designed for family life

When Antony inherited the house in 1889 he employed architect Henry Woodyer to make a number of practical changes to the Hall, altering its layout and moving the main staircase to the west wall. These changes created extra space on the ground floor, which was used as an informal living area by Antony's family. Nowadays at Christmas, a decorated tree adds sparkle and colour, conjuring up images of Victorian family celebrations.

Below **The Hall**

3 The Library

Although it contains a superb collection of books that reflect the Gibbs family's interests, the Library was not just a place to store and study books. It was designed by Norton to also be a family sitting room for William and Blanche. Their children, and Antony's, used to put on plays and other performances here, using the bay window area as their stage. Antony's son George brought in the fine porcelain and Georgian-style furniture.

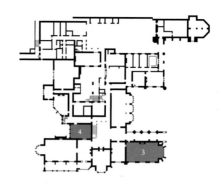

The best of British

The British Library classifies Tyntesfield's Library as the top grade, Grade 5, considering it an outstanding example of a Victorian gentleman's library. It contains around 2,000 books, purchased by four generations of the Gibbs family. The books cover a wide range of subjects including theology, science, fine art, history, poetry and gardening.

Good housekeeping

The sofa and chairs with gold covers date from about 1855. William commissioned them from the leading Victorian decorators and furnishers Crace & Sons. They have always had 'slip' (loose) covers to protect their delicate wool and silk fabric. It was, and is, the practical way to look after high-quality furniture. The carpet was hand-made for this room.

Left The Library as arranged by George and Via, c.1912

Right The fireplace is a bold statement of High Victorian Gothic

4 The Organ Room

This room was specifically designed by William's architect John Norton as an oratory, a private devotional space for the family and household. William and Blanche were committed Christians and were profoundly influenced by the High Church Oxford Movement. Religion was central to their lives and Tyntesfield's day started and ended with prayers for the family and servants. In William's time, before the Chapel was built, daily prayers were held in this room.

Some time after the Chapel was built, Antony converted the oratory into an organ room, installing a large organ that he played regularly. He added the carved double doors as soundproofing. George, 1st Lord Wraxall, converted the Organ Room into an office for his secretary, and it was subsequently used by the house secretary.

The Oxford Movement and the Tractarians
The Oxford Movement originated in that city in 1833 when the Reverend John Keble criticised government interference in the Church of England. Keble and others published a series of religious papers, *Tracts for the Times* (a copy is in the Library), calling for reform and a return to the Church's Catholic roots. Their supporters – among them William and Blanche and famous figures such as poet Christina Rossetti and Prime Minister William Gladstone – were known as Tractarians. Tractarians encouraged a revival of traditional forms of worship, music, vestments and fittings, and championed architecture, decoration and furnishings with religious symbolism. Oxford Movement ideas influenced the design of many Victorian Gothic Revival churches, with ornamented altars, rich decoration and stained glass. Keble College, Oxford, was established in 1870, having been built as a monument to John Keble. Its hall and chapel were funded by a large donation from William.

Gentlemen's rooms

There were distinct divisions within Victorian country houses, with some areas of the house used predominantly by men, some used mainly by women, and others used by both but considered to be more masculine or feminine in character.

This division reflected social structures and the lifestyles of wealthy families at the time: the owner directed the management of the estate, while his wife was in charge of household matters, formal entertaining and childcare. This in turn was a key element in the design of Victorian country houses, as is strikingly evident at Tyntesfield. The Oak Room, Dining Room and Billiard Room were all considered to be primarily masculine spaces. The Drawing Room, Morning Room and former Mrs Gibbs's Room were predominantly for the ladies of the house. Twentieth-century changes altered the distinctions.

5 The Oak Room

All four generations of Tyntesfield gentlemen used the Oak Room as their office or study. In the 1866 plans for Tyntesfield published in *The Builder* journal, this room was called Mr Gibbs's Room. When Antony inherited he also used it as his private retreat, and the alterations he had made by his architect Henry Woodyer reflect his taste for fine craftsmanship. Woodyer installed new oak panelling and cupboards, one of which is actually the door through to the Morning Room (the Music Room on the 1866 plans). When George died, his second wife, Ursula, used the Oak Room as her office and as a sitting room. After her death, the room became Richard's office and sitting room, filled with his paintings and ornaments as well as family photographs and papers. It was one of the very few rooms in the house that was in regular use when Richard died in 2001.

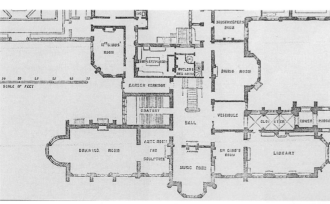

Left Floorplans published in *The Builder* (1866) show the Oak Room as 'Mr Gibbs's Room' and the Dining Room before alteration with its single bay window

Right Fine wood carving in the Oak Room

Far right The imitation-leather wallpaper was one of Antony's additions

6 The Dining Room

This is one of Tyntesfield's most important reception rooms, where the family and guests would have eaten their meals every day. It was in continuous use from William's time right up until Richard, 2nd Lord Wraxall's death in 2001. Like most Victorian dining rooms, it has a strongly masculine feel. This room was probably part of the original Regency house bought by William in 1843. It was remodelled by William's architect John Norton during his major rebuilding work between 1863 and 1865. Norton designed a new fireplace but the lower half of the great sideboard, which had been commissioned from Crace in the 1850s, was retained.

Woodyer's reworking

In William's day the Dining Room was smaller, with one wide bay window. In 1889-90 Antony's architect Henry Woodyer extended it lengthways into what had been the housekeeper's room and widened it, adding three bay windows. He moved Norton's fireplace so that it remained in the centre of the wall and added the mirror and surround. The eastern-style carpet was specially made to fit around the stone columns. The room was redecorated with embossed and gilded imitation-leather wallpaper that survives to this day. It would seem Antony was proud of the remodelling of this room, as he had his initials carved above the columns.

The cornflakes pig
The pig tureen was given to Richard, 2nd Lord Wraxall, by his brother Eustace. Richard stored his cornflakes in it.

The gentlemen's suite

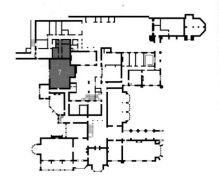

Tyntesfield's Billiard Room and adjacent Lathe Room, Gun Room and Gentlemen's Lavatory were all part of William's major rebuilding of the house in the 1860s, undertaken by John Norton and then improved by Henry Woodyer.

Together these rooms are a fine example of a Victorian gentlemen's suite. Gun rooms for storing and cleaning guns became more common in the later half of the 19th century as shooting parties grew in popularity. Tyntesfield was one of the first Victorian houses to have a gun room linked with the Billiard Room.

Below The electric scoreboard for the billiard table

7 The Billiard Room

Most Victorian country houses had a billiard room. When William had his built he had four teenaged sons and its location away from the main rooms of the house may have been a deliberate decision. He also created the Lathe Room for Antony, who was a fine craftsman and created beautiful objects made of turned wood and ivory.

Hunting trophies

George and his first wife Via loved to travel and were fond of shooting and fishing. They often went shooting in Scotland and visited Russia and North America on shooting expeditions. The large moose above the fireplace was shot by Via in 1911.

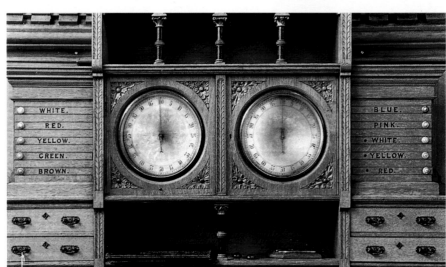

The billiard table

The billiard table was specially made for Antony in 1884 and was originally installed at Charlton House (see page 5). It is an amazing piece of craftsmanship, made by James Plucknett & Co. Constructed in oak, it has 12 panels with carvings showing traditional British sports such as archery, bowls and wrestling. It also incorporated the latest technology. The slate bed was heated by hot water pipes beneath the table and the table was linked to a separate scoring board by electrical wires. Players pushed the buttons on the table to record their scores.

The billiard table was moved to Tyntesfield when Antony inherited the house. It may have been brought into this room when Henry Woodyer made the opening in the east wall to create the inglenook fireplace. The billiard table has been here ever since. It is one of the few pieces of furniture that hasn't been moved for decades, due to its weight.

'When his Lordship renovated the Billiard Room in 1995, I had to arrange for two sets of scaffolding, one over the roof and another smaller set over the billiard table. We couldn't move the table because it is connected to the central heating system.'

Ray Llewellyn, former Estate Manager, 2011

Left The Billiard Room

Ladies' rooms

The Morning Room and what is now Lord Wraxall's Sitting Room were rooms for the principal use of the ladies of Tyntesfield, from which they might oversee the running of the household, and in which they might also relax, read and catch up on their correspondence.

8 The Morning Room

South facing, this room used as an informal sitting room catches all the morning light and has lovely views out over the Terraces to the parkland. It was part of the original Regency house that William bought in 1843. His architect John Norton added the Gothic fireplace and enlarged the bay window as part of his rebuilding work in 1863–65. The room is marked as the Music Room on the 1866 house plans and we know that Blanche played her harp here.

When Antony inherited he altered the layout of the Morning Room, blocking the door to the Hall and inserting new doors to the Oak and Ante Rooms. He commissioned a new carpet, which was hand-made to fit the room. He had his initials woven into the corners, just as his father had done with the carpet in the Drawing Room.

Janet, Antony's wife, used this room until her death. After 1907, it became George and Via's family sitting room. Later Ursula used it as her office and sitting room. When she died in 1979, her son Richard closed the shutters and covered the furniture. They are still closed today to protect the fragile carpet and furnishings.

Victorian ventilation
There are two upright ducting pipes on either side of the bay window that ventilate the room. Preventing stale or 'vitiated' air was a widespread concern among Victorian households and the Gibbses had a ventilation system installed to ensure a supply of fresh air. The vents are opened by little hand-shaped handles.

Below left Blanche with her harp when the Morning Room was known as the Music Room

Below A frieze of elaborately carved and naturalistic motifs runs around what was Blanche's sitting room

9 Lord Wraxall's Sitting Room (formerly Mrs Gibbs's Room)

The Victorian counterpart to Mr Gibbs's Room (now the Oak Room), this was designed as Blanche's private space away from the formal rooms. The room was probably part of the original house that William Gibbs bought in 1843. You can see what the original house looked like in the framed picture on the wall. John Norton added the arched door to lead to his great conservatory. But the conservatory had to be demolished after storm damage in 1916, and the garden porch was built in its place.

Changing rooms

When Antony inherited the house after Blanche's death, his wife Janet used this as her sitting room. George and his son Richard both used it as a business room. It was furnished with a table and desks, chairs and sofas, probably much as it is now. The bookshelves contain some of the books bought and used by Richard, 2nd Lord Wraxall and reflect his interest in forestry and wildlife.

Beautiful boxwood

Intricately detailed roses, strawberries and pineapples are some of the naturalistic carvings of flowers and fruits on the panelling in Mrs Gibbs's Room, added after the room was redesigned for Blanche. Family tradition says that the frieze of boxwood carvings at the top of the panelling was done by Antony, who was a highly skilled craftsman.

Above The house before John Norton's remodelling, or *A View of the South Front of Tyntes Place*, attributed to H. Hewitt

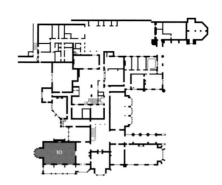

10 The Drawing Room

This is Tyntesfield's grandest reception room, used in the afternoon and evening and for formal parties and receptions. It was designed by Norton to balance the Library, the other new room that he added to the south front of the house. It is a large room, more than 40 foot (12 metres) long and rising into the roof, overlooking the south terraces and the lawns of the formal garden. We know exactly how it looked in William and Blanche's day, as it was photographed by Bedford Lemere in 1878 soon after William's death. It was a splendid Victorian room, very much the ladies' domain, richly but lightly and colourfully decorated with hand-painted and stencilled walls (surviving decoration of red, light green and gold was found behind wall hangings in 2009). There were upholstered chairs and a huge mirror over a Gothic fireplace, all supplied by Crace & Sons.

Edwardian tastes

George and Via redecorated and updated the Drawing Room when they moved into Tyntesfield in 1907 to play down its, by then, unfashionable Gothic style. They furnished it in the Venetian palazzo style, changing the colour scheme to deep reds, dyeing the original carpet and covering the stencilled walls with crimson damask wall hangings. They also replaced the original Crace fireplace with a new one made of Carrara marble, commissioned in Venice, and introduced real and high-quality reproduction 17th- and 18th-century furniture.

Disappearing doors

The doors to the Drawing Room were cleverly designed with entertainment in mind. They have normal hinges as well as a sliding mechanism that allows them to be pushed back into the wall. With the doors hidden away the Drawing Room and adjacent Ante Room effectively become a single space – perfect for parties.

Top Bedford Lemere's photograph of the Drawing Room taken in 1878

Opposite The Drawing Room today

Upstairs

The upper floors of Tyntesfield provided bedrooms and service space for the family, their guests and staff. Many of the original fittings installed by William and then Antony are still in place, along with additions by George and Via, Ursula and finally a few changes made by Richard, the last Gibbs to live here.

The principal family and guest bedrooms are on the first floor overlooking the entrance forecourt, terraces and gardens. The nurseries and lesser family and guest bedrooms are on the second floor. Service rooms, store rooms, servants' living rooms and bedrooms are mostly in the service wing on the north side.

Ascending to the first floor
In William's day the family reached the first floor by a central T-shaped staircase from the Hall, which divided to reach the gallery. The servants used the back stairs on the other side of the wall. Antony's alterations moved the stairs to their current position against the wall, leading to the gallery that stretches around almost three sides of the room. The back stairs were moved to their current position. The upper floors were also served by a hydraulic lift, a fascinating piece of Victorian technology. Installed around 1890 (Queen Victoria installed one at Balmoral in 1893), it was originally powered by water. It was a service rather than a passenger lift, used for coal and other heavy loads.

Opposite The stairs were moved to their current position as a part of Antony's alterations

Twenty-two colours
The carpet on the stairs and gallery floors was made in 2010. It looks just like the Victorian 1890 chenille carpet, which was in shreds when the National Trust took over the house. Specialist carpet makers adapted modern techniques to create the new one as the original chenille technique is no longer available, using 22 colours to replicate the original carpet.

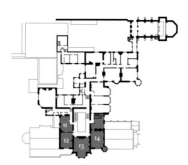

11 Lord Wraxall's Bedroom

This was Richard, 2nd Lord Wraxall's bedroom. He moved into it as a teenager, when he left the nursery, and he used it all his adult life. Perhaps he kept it as his bedroom for the wonderful views it has over the clipped hollies of the Broad Walk as far as Paradise.

12 Mr Gibbs's Bedroom

Eustace, the current and 3rd Lord Wraxall, had this bedroom when he lived at Tyntesfield in the 1930s and 40s and always used it when he came home to visit his mother and brother. Like Lord Wraxall's bedroom, this was part of the original 1820s house, little altered by William's and Antony's rebuilding and improvements, other than being redecorated, most recently in the early 1900s for Via, George's first wife. The green decorative scheme and the marble fireplace were installed for her soon after 1907, when George inherited the house. This may have been her boudoir, a private sitting room next to the Stuart Bedroom.

A good timekeeper

In the last few years of his life, Richard had three clocks in his bedroom, one on the wall and two beside his bed to make sure that he was in time for early business meetings.

13 The Stuart Room

This was Via's bedroom and its furniture and decoration reflect her tastes with a mix of Dutch and Italian marquetry antiques and Edwardian mahogany. This blending of antique and reproduction furniture was in vogue in Edwardian times and is evident here and in the Drawing Room. Both rooms were redesigned and decorated during George and Via's time. The white marble fireplace survives from the original 1820s house.

14 The Charlton Room and Bathroom

This was probably Blanche's bedroom until she died in 1887. The turret was added by Norton as part of his rebuilding of the original 1820s house. The adjoining bathroom was originally a dressing room and was probably converted by Antony's architect Woodyer when he modernised the house. It was for many years the only en-suite bathroom in the house.

Fashions of the time

The Gothic fireplace is typical of those installed by John Norton in 1863–65. The decorative tiles surrounding the fireplace were covered with dark paint sometime in the 20th century, possibly when Ursula used this room as her bedroom in the 1970s.

Opposite The Charlton Room seen from its adjoining turret

Above The brown and white fish motif on the tiles of the Charlton Bathroom

Left The Stuart Room

Below stairs

The butler and the housekeeper were the most important servants. There was a strict hierarchy of responsibilities from the highest servant to the most lowly. The lowliest servants, such as scullery maids or the hall boy, might never venture out of their part of the servants' wing. Both Norton and Woodyer planned the servants' wing for maximum efficiency, grouping together the rooms of the various departments.

The 1891 Census records Antony and Janet living at Tyntesfield with their nine children and 19 domestic servants: the butler and two footmen, the housekeeper, a lady's maid, cook, six housemaids, nurse, two nursery maids, stillroom maid, two scullery maids and a hall boy.

Everyone had their daily tasks, and Tyntesfield's architects remodelled with the day-to-day running of the household in mind. John Norton demolished part of the servants' wing of the original 1820 house, replacing it with new larger buildings fitted with the latest technology. Antony, in turn, modernised the servants' wing, introducing electricity and the lift, adding storage space and changing the layout of the butler's and housekeeper's rooms. The 19th-century fittings survive, although most of the decoration is 20th century.

The butler's department

The butler was in charge of the silver and the wine cellar and managed the male servants. In 1898–99 Woodyer converted Norton's butler's pantry into a plate scullery with a safe for storing the silver. The scullery has a lead-lined sink to reduce the risk of denting the silver plate when being washed. The butler's bedroom became the new butler's pantry. It has a teak sink for washing glassware and a rack for draining decanters. Silver continued to be cleaned in this room until Lord Wraxall's death in 2001.

The housekeeper's department

The housekeeper was responsible for furniture and linen, buying, storing and distributing provisions. She was in charge of the female staff. She controlled the still room with its range and special oven where cakes and preserves were made and afternoon tea was prepared. In 1889 Woodyer converted the housekeeper's stores to a new housekeeper's room. It was her office and a living room for the most important servants, who ate all or some of their meals here. It was also a store room, and still is – table linen and fine dinner services are still in the cupboards. In the 20th century it became the staff room after the servants' hall was abandoned. Now volunteers use this room to conserve the collections, and you may see them at work here.

Left House staff in the late 19th century. Seated by the dog is Hemmings, who remained in service until the 1940s

The cook's department

The kitchen was the most important room in the servants' wing. Tyntesfield's kitchen is much closer to the Dining Room than was usual in most Victorian country houses. It has iron windows and a high fire-proof vaulted ceiling and it faces north which helps to keep it cool. Unusually, it has remained in continuous use ever since it was built. The microwave and wine cooler were Richard, 2nd Lord Wraxall's additions. In the early years of opening to the public, National Trust staff and volunteers cooked and ate here, even when the room was open to visitors.

The bells

Every Victorian country house had bells to summon servants. Tyntesfield's hang on springs linked by a complex system of pulleys and wires to bell handles in all the family rooms. Servants would get to know the sounds of different bells and the indicator swings for several minutes. If you look carefully you can see different writing where the names of rooms have changed over time.

Left Cut-glass decanters with tins and groceries in the housekeeper's stores

The Chapel

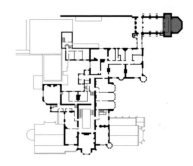

The Chapel is the architectural climax of the house. It was not unusual for a Victorian country house to have a chapel and this is one of the finest – a superb Victorian Gothic creation that has survived virtually unchanged since it was completed in 1875.

Tyntesfield's Chapel was commissioned and built in the last two years of William's life, between 1873 and 1875. It can be considered a symbol of his spiritual journey and the climax of the house, a glorious and richly decorated private chapel built on a grand scale for a devout Christian family. The journey through the Chapel is highly symbolic, approaching the altar with increasing height and light, parallelled by increasingly elaborate and intricate decoration. The altar is the focal point of the Chapel, surrounded by soaring Devonshire marble pillars. The altar was particularly important for Tractarians (see page 25), as the site where the sacrament of Holy Communion takes place.

A devout family
Religion was central to the lives of William and Blanche and their children. It guided every aspect of their lives, from the way they spent their time and money to the way they cared for their servants and tenants.

Inspired design
Although the Chapel now dominates any view of the house, it was not part of John Norton's major rebuild of 1863–65. It was added a decade later, by architect Arthur Blomfield. It is a clever and inspired design based on the medieval La Sainte Chapelle in Paris, elegantly solving the triple challenge of a small and awkwardly shaped site at the entrance to the servants' courtyard on steeply sloping ground.

Blomfield created an undercroft at ground level, which raised the Chapel to a similar level as the first floor of the house. The chaplain, the family and their guests went to the Chapel for morning and evening prayers and services via a corridor and bridge on the first floor. Servants entered the Chapel by a spiral staircase from the courtyard and the estate staff used the exterior door off the North Drive.

Opposite Arthur Blomfield's Gothic Chapel modelled on the medieval La Sainte Chapelle, Paris

Arthur Blomfield
William's appointed chapel architect designed many churches. He was the son of a Bishop of London who initiated a programme of church building in the capital. Blomfield was highly regarded both as an architect and as a restorer of historic buildings. As well as churches and chapels, he designed for colleges and schools. He had a large architectural practice and one of his apprentices was the writer Thomas Hardy.

+ SAINT + PAVL

Licensed for prayer

When the Chapel was designed, the undercroft was intended to be a crypt for family burials. However the vicar of Wraxall objected and the Bishop of Bath and Wells did not allow the Chapel to be consecrated, so funerals, weddings and Matins continued to be held at Wraxall's church. However, morning and evening prayers and Holy Communion were held daily in the Chapel during William's and Antony's time, after Blanche requested a licence from the Bishop. Special licences have subsequently been granted for marriages, funerals and commemorative services. Doreen, Richard's half-sister, was married in the Chapel and her memorial service took place here in 2008. The present Lord Wraxall was christened in the Chapel, as were two of his children, and services are held here each year.

In memory

The elegant communion set of chalice and altar flagon for communion wine was made soon after William's death. It was commissioned by Blanche in his memory and is delicately inlaid with rubies, sapphires, opals and emeralds that he had given her during their marriage.

There are crosses to commemorate 14 members of the Gibbs family, dating from William's death in 1875 through to Richard, 2nd Lord Wraxall, who died in 2001.

'The detail in the mosaic faces behind the altar is amazing – even the wrinkles on their faces are separate tiles.'

Ruth Moppett, Inventory
Supervisor, 2011

Left The subject and quality of the Chapel's mosaics reflect its supreme purpose

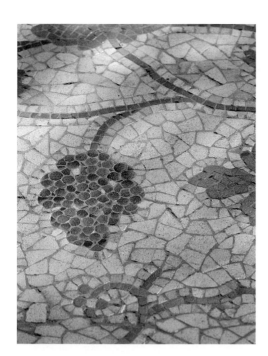

Detailed mosaics

The mosaics on the floor and behind the altar were designed by Blomfield. The floor mosaic increases in richness, both in colour and in the materials used, as the altar is approached, where squares of a rare Derbyshire Bluejohn mineral replace the honey-coloured Mexican onyx used for most of the floor. The glittering mosaics behind the altar were probably commissioned from and installed by the Venice and Murano Glass and Mosaic Company.

Glass that glows

The exceptional stained-glass windows in the Chapel were designed by two of the leading designers of the 1870s: Harry Ellis Wooldridge designed the glass in the main part of the Chapel; James Croft Powell designed the magnificent rose window above the organ gallery. The original organ was carefully constructed with graduated pipes so that the window was not obscured. The family had the organ removed from the Chapel after the Second World War so that it could be used to supply replacement parts for organs in Bristol churches that had been damaged in bombing raids.

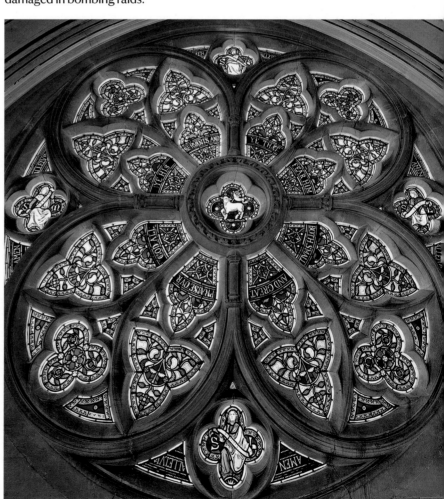

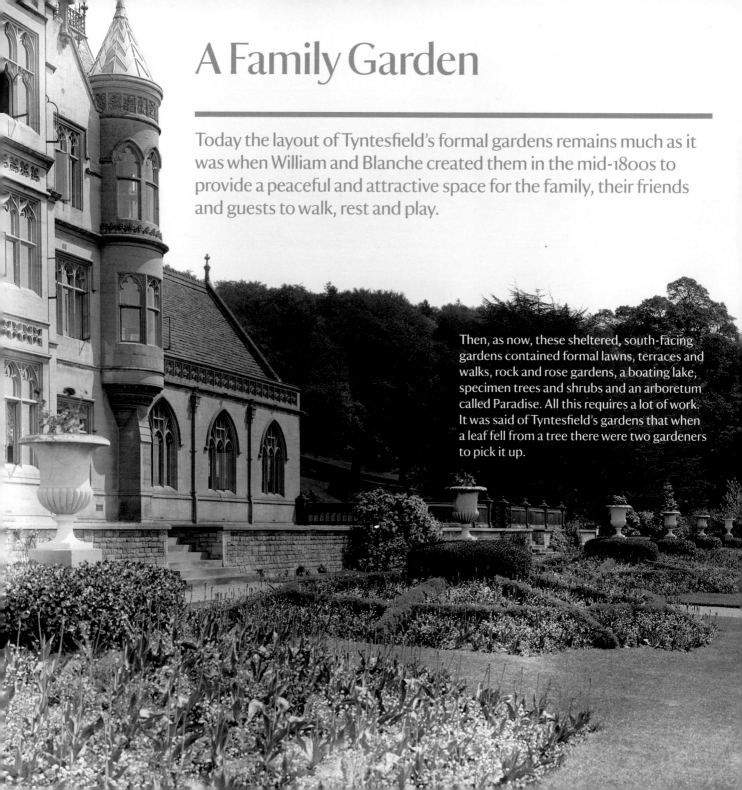

A Family Garden

Today the layout of Tyntesfield's formal gardens remains much as it was when William and Blanche created them in the mid-1800s to provide a peaceful and attractive space for the family, their friends and guests to walk, rest and play.

Then, as now, these sheltered, south-facing gardens contained formal lawns, terraces and walks, rock and rose gardens, a boating lake, specimen trees and shrubs and an arboretum called Paradise. All this requires a lot of work. It was said of Tyntesfield's gardens that when a leaf fell from a tree there were two gardeners to pick it up.

The Terraces

The Terraces were created in the 1850s. In the 1860s Gothic stone seats were added, probably designed by John Norton who rebuilt Tyntesfield for William and Blanche in the 1860s. The paths were gravelled so the Terraces could be used throughout the year. Antony made improvements when he inherited, making the Terraces more formal as was fashionable in the 1880s.

Restoration of the garden

The planting of the formal garden remains much as it was in the early 1900s, when Antony and then his son George were in charge of Tyntesfield. The garden was perhaps at its peak at this time, carefully tended by an army of gardeners. The gardens were occasionally opened for local events such as the Nailsea and District Flower Show and village fêtes.

Historic shrubs, climbers and flowers such as pomegranate, myrtle, rose, wisteria and lemon verbena were still growing in the gardens when the National Trust came in 2002. Many were over mature, but an ambitious yet cautious pruning programme is returning these plants to their former glory.

The Portugal Laurel Walk was replanted in 2011, with cuttings grown from the original trees. As the laurels mature, they will be clipped into domes, restoring the walk to its original appearance.

Tiny orchids

Autumn Ladies Tresses orchids grow in the lawn of the topmost terrace. The small white flowers appear in August and September. As soon as the orchids' leaves appear in the lawn in July, all mowing stops in that area and does not start until the flowers have set their seeds.

Opposite The Terraces photographed in 1902

Above The Terraces today

Left Autumn Ladies Tresses orchids are an unusual and welcome treat on the Terraces in late summer

Formal features

The Terraces and Broad Walk run east to west, along the contours of the valley and are linked by stone steps. These features were created around the same time as the Rose Garden and Paradise, all with as much thought and care as the design of the house.

The Broad Walk

The Broad Walk dates from the 1850s. It is flanked by pairs of specimen holly trees, thought to be at least 130 years old. Every year in October these trees are carefully clipped into mushroom-shaped domes, each one taking about an hour and a half to do.

The Broad Walk leads you out from the centre of the west face of the house to a large carved, curved stone seat with lovely views out over the valley towards the north Somerset coast.

Above The clipped hollies of the Broad Walk are over a century old

Left The stone seat was designed by John Norton

The conservatory

Up until 1916 there was a splendid conservatory at the northwest corner of the house, adjoining Mrs Gibbs's Room and the Billiard Room. It was designed by John Norton and was a huge and impressive structure. It was 80 foot (24 metres) long, 50 foot (15 metres) wide and topped by a 50-foot (15-metre) dome with a gilt-copper cupola, modelled on that of St Mark's Cathedral in Venice. It was heated by an underground boiler. Rainwater from the roof was collected for use in the house and also to supply the Boating Lake. Sadly the conservatory had to be demolished after a severe winter storm damaged the dome beyond repair. Luckily we can see exactly how it looked in numerous photographs taken between the 1860s and 1900s. You can still see the footprint of the conservatory outside the house, between the start of the Broad Walk and the west window of the Billiard Room.

The Aviary

This is a rare survivor of a once popular Victorian garden feature. It was probably built between 1867 and 1883 for William and Blanche and housed small exotic birds. Via converted it into a playhouse for her daughter Doreen, and they often used it for dolls' tea parties. Richard and Eustace kept budgerigars in it.

When the Trust came to Tyntesfield, the Aviary was in a state of collapse and needed emergency propping. Parts of the timber frame had rotted away and the front of the building had fallen in on itself. Specialist staff worked out how it had been made and found many of the original components inside. Skilled craftsmen repaired it in 2011 but it was a challenge: 'It was like a jigsaw puzzle – all the broken bits were stored inside the remains of the building. We had to get them all out and see out how they all went together before we could start repairing the broken or rotten pieces.'

Top left The grand but now-vanished conservatory with dome modelled on that of St Mark's Cathedral, Venice

Above A fancy-dress party in the conservatory about 1900

Below left The recently restored Aviary

The Rose Garden

Tyntesfield's Rose Garden is accessed from the Broad Walk, enclosed by trees and Gothic stone walls, and approached by a set of stone steps guarded by lions. It was part of the original garden designed for William and Blanche in the 1850s.

Despite its name, the Rose Garden has only a few roses as the local deer tend to eat them. The rose beds have box hedging and old-fashioned scented roses grow on the iron pergola. Two timber and stone gazebos overlook the garden, offering sheltered seating with views over the garden, and in the past, before the garden's trees matured, open and extensive views over the valley of the Land Yeo River, towards the Mendip Hills and the Bristol Channel. The gazebos were derelict when the Trust arrived and were restored in 2008–09.

Remake and repair
The tiles on the walls and floors of the gazebos were made by Minton, the leading decorative tile manufacturers of the Victorian era. Many were broken or missing when the National Trust acquired Tyntesfield in 2002, but piles of tiles were discovered stacked behind the gazebos, completely overgrown by vegetation. Specialist conservators have restored these tiles and created new ones to return the gazebos to their former charm.

Above The view from the Rose Garden over the stone lions standing guard

The Rock Gardens

Rock gardens or rockeries were fashionable in Victorian times, particularly after substantial rockeries were created at Edinburgh in the 1870s and at Kew in 1882.

There were two rock gardens during the 'glory days' of Tyntesfield's formal gardens in the late 1800s and early 1900s, one along the western banks of the Boating Lake and the other at the edges of the Rose Garden. Both were key elements, adding large, naturalistic features, new textures and planting opportunities as well as year-round colour and interest.

'We found hundreds of Victorian metal plant labels for exotic and ornamental trees and shrubs on the estate…. They give a tantalising hint of what may have been planted here and indicate more exciting and colourful planting schemes.'

Paul Evans, Head Gardener, 2011

Left The gazebo has been reclaimed from the greenery and restored to glory

Right Hundreds of Victorian ceramic and metal plant labels tell us what the Gibbses grew

The leisure garden

There is much evidence in the house of a closely bonded family that prayed together daily. On the lawns around the house where the Gibbses would stroll, picnic and enjoy games such as croquet and tennis, a family that played together is also evident.

The lawns

The lawns have always been an important feature of Tyntesfield, enhancing the setting of the house and offering open views from the Drawing Room and other rooms on the west front as well as space for family and guests to enjoy walking, cycling and all sorts of games.

Above, below and opposite
The Croquet Lawn has always been a popular spot with visitors, especially for family games and picnics

'The lake held water up until 1939 when it was drained to prevent enemy aircraft using it for navigation. It was dry for most of the war and the concrete cracked. It always leaked after that and was dry for many years. We filled half of it with water for Lord Wraxall's 60th birthday party in 1988 – it looked fantastic!'

Ray Llewellyn, former Estate Manager, 2011

Anyone for tennis?

Old photographs show the family and guests playing tennis on the lawn now used for croquet. The grassy banks around the hard tennis courts are full of traditional meadow flora such as bird's foot trefoil, wild thyme and clover, indicating that the ground has not been treated with artificial fertilisers. We manage these grassy areas as traditional hay meadows, leaving the plants to flower and produce seed before cutting. The cut grass is spread on nearby fields, to improve their biodiversity.

Jewels in the grass

The lawns are also important for wildlife. As well as lots of delicate wildflowers and grasses, the lawn is also home to groups of rare fungi, especially waxcaps. These colourful and unusual fungi are only found in old grassland that has not been improved. They appear in the autumn, usually between October and December, and the different varieties have a wonderful range of colours from pale pink and white through to brilliant yellow, bright scarlet and dark purple.

The Boating Lake

This artificial lake was probably created by William Gibbs in the 1870s possibly from an existing farm pond. It was filled with rainwater from the roofs of the conservatory via an ingenious system of underground pipes and tanks. It was a very shallow lake and, although extensive, the water supply was always rather erratic. A huge metal plug in the deepest part of the lake allowed it to be drained. Large pieces of rock around the western banks of the Boating Lake are the remnants of a former rock garden.

Below Guests on the Boating Lake drained in 1939 and never refilled

Paradise

Gardening on the wild side
Tyntesfield's Library contains several books by William Robinson – an influential Irish Victorian journalist whose most popular book was called *The Wild Garden*. He advocated a more naturalistic approach to gardening, a reaction to the 'vulgar' bedding displays so popular in the 19th century. Some estate records refer to Paradise as 'The Wild Garden', and its planting may have been influenced by Robinson.

This evocatively named garden is an arboretum with a collection of specimen trees at the western end of the Broad Walk. The family called it Paradise, perhaps because of its peaceful atmosphere and groups of beautiful trees, perhaps because some of the cedars are grown from seeds brought back from the Holy Land in 1858.

The arboretum was probably created by William towards the end of his life, perhaps with Blanche and Antony. It is marked on the Ordnance Survey map of 1883.

Creating an arboretum was fashionable amongst wealthy landowners. Plant collecting was a popular hobby for many wealthy Victorians, and major plant nurseries funded specialist plant collectors to travel the world, especially North America and China, seeking out unusual plants to bring back to Britain, sometimes as mature trees, more often as seeds and seedlings. This was the golden era of plant collecting and resulted in Victorian gardeners having an amazing range of new plants to add colour, shape and height to their gardens and landscapes.

Below Paradise is an example of a Victorian arboretum, a showcase for specimen trees

The parkland

There are two areas of parkland at Tyntesfield, to the south and west of the gardens, giving the house and gardens a pastoral setting. Many of the trees were planted around 1860, in William's time, as part of his development of the house and grounds.

The parkland has clumps of oak, lime, Wellingtonia, Blue Cedar and Cedar of Lebanon. Some of the planting is contemporary with the 1820 house, and much more was added by the Gibbs family in the 19th century and later.

To the east of the drive there was an area of small fields in 1837. This was largely converted to parkland around 1860, removing a public road, and the holly hedge to the current road was planted as the park boundary. Some of the ornamental clumps of trees remain, but others have been lost, opening up unintended views towards the Kitchen Garden.

All four generations of the Gibbses planted trees in the parkland, and after William's time new trees were added for both their aesthetic appeal and as a commercial crop. The age and variety of Tyntesfield's parkland trees adds significantly to the biodiversity of the estate.

Above The parkland viewed from the house

Tyntesfield Today

Sustainability lies at the heart of all our work. We look after special places for everyone, for ever. We have a responsibility to sustain our properties, managing them for future generations to enjoy, and at the same time protecting our precious natural environment.

Building in sustainability

Tyntesfield, like all our historic houses and properties, needs heat and electricity to function, and we are committed to producing and using this energy as responsibly as we can.

Reducing our use of fossil fuels

Back in 2008 we explained our ambition to reduce our use of fossil fuels by 50 per cent by 2020, and the repair and restoration of the house and the conversion of Home Farm buildings to visitor facilities gave us excellent opportunities to use new energy conservation and production technologies.

But using modern technology isn't a new approach at Tyntesfield – both William and Antony Gibbs fitted the latest energy systems of their day, William when he was creating the house and Antony when he was updating it.

New technologies

We've added state of the art insulation to the roofs of the house and Home Farm buildings, installed biomass boilers and photovoltaic systems for heat and fitted a clever lighting control system which automatically dims or brightens the lights at Home Farm, according to the amount of natural light available. We recycle rainwater to flush toilets and our hand driers are super-efficient to save electricity.

Raising the roof

Most of the buildings at Home Farm have tiled roofs, and many needed replacing during the conversion work to create new visitor facilities. We cleaned, sorted and reused tiles that were stored around the estate. When the former covered yards for cattle were converted into a shop and restaurant, we inserted a layer of very thin multifoil insulation above the roof rafters. We needed Listed Building Consent because the insulation raised the roofline by 55 mm. The extra height is cleverly disguised by specially designed details at the eaves and gutters.

Green gardening

Tyntesfield's gardeners are doing their bit for sustainability by adding the ash from the biomass boilers to their compost. They also recycle all the green waste from the estate in the garden and make their own organic liquid fertilizer from comfrey grown in the Kitchen Garden. Future plans include a purpose-built composter so we can recycle all the food waste from the restaurant and cafés.

Opposite **Not the only visitors: a 2011 survey recorded 779 different kinds of plants and animals living at Tyntesfield**

Above **Home Farm buildings converted into visitor facilities in 2011**

Below **Produce grown in the Kitchen Garden, for sale at Tyntesfield**

Continuing conservation

In April 2002 we launched a campaign to save Tyntesfield. Just 50 days later, £24 million had been raised, with a grant of £17.4m from the National Heritage Memorial Fund and over £8m in public donations.

This was the start of a long-term programme to conserve and restore this magnificent Victorian house and its supporting buildings, gardens and estate. Right from the start we've been determined that as many people as possible should benefit from Tyntesfield. We've involved people from a wide range of backgrounds and abilities and thousands of volunteers, life-long learners, students and trainees have enjoyed the special opportunities Tyntesfield has to offer. Generous funding from the Heritage Lottery Fund has enabled us to carry out essential repairs and to adapt the estate for full public enjoyment and access. We've repaired the roof of the house and Chapel and renewed all the plumbing and electrical wiring. There are new visitor facilities at Home Farm, where the animal stalls and milking parlour have been converted into a new restaurant and shop, and we've made a new learning centre in the Sawmill. But there is still more to do, so make sure you come again to find out what's new!

Right Hundreds of people have so far been involved in restoring Tyntesfield. Ask how you can get involved